DATE DUE

1998			
OCT 8			
OCT 24			
2000			
NOV 1			
2002			
OCT 1 2003			
MAY 19 2004			
JUN 25 2005			
OCT 14 2005			
3-23			
11/1/13			

Demco, Inc. 38-293

FABULOUS
Fun
Costumes

Fun Costumes

Juliet Moxley

Sterling Publishing Co., Inc.
New York

For Alice and Jessica

Library of Congress
Cataloging-in-Publication Data Available

2 4 6 8 10 9 7 5 3 1

Published in 1997 by Sterling Publishing Company, Inc.
387 Park Avenue South, New York, N.Y. 10016

Originally published in Great Britain in 1996 by Ebury Press
as *The Complete Book of Dressing Up*
Text © 1996 Juliet Moxley
Photography © 1996 Ebury Press

Distributed in Canada by Sterling Publishing
c/o Canadian Manda Group, One Atlantic Avenue, Suite 105
Toronto, Ontario, Canada M6K 3E7

Printed and bound in Portugal

9/21/98

Sterling ISBN 0-8069-9852-0

CONTENTS

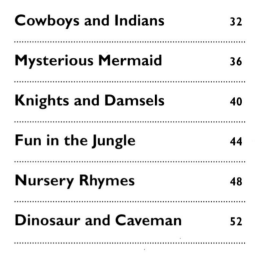

INTRODUCTION

Children of all ages love dressing up. They might be going to a costume party or simply want to play in a make-believe world. Whatever the occasion, "pretending" or acting out an adventure is much more fun if you are wearing the right disguise. Younger children in particular love to hear their parents say, "I can't see so-and-so anywhere, but who's this handsome cowboy?"

Of course, it is possible to buy costumes, but these are often expensive, especially if you have more than one child. This book is full of costumes that are easy and inexpensive to make. I am qualified to write it because I am a working mother with four children who have all wanted to dress up as something or other over the last fifteen years. I have had lots of practice at creating outfits!

You can make many of the costumes using old sheets, curtains, worn-out clothes, or scraps of material. Some take a little time to make, but you don't need to be an expert with a sewing machine for all the costumes. For instance, if you don't want to make a complete animal body out of fake fur (using the all-in-one pattern that can be adapted to make almost any costume), your child will feel just as dressed up wearing leggings or tights and a top in the same color, together with a tail and perhaps a hood with animal ears.

I have also included some props that complete the picture and that children can help with. Fairies need magic wands with glittery stars on top and butterflies can have wings decorated with shapes cut out of colored paper. You can easily make a glittering crown or cheerful clown's hat once you know how. Costume parties are often the reason that children dress up, so I have suggested a few games and things for children to do while they are in their costumes – it all adds to the fun.

Getting Started

Before you begin to make a costume, think about what is involved, what is going to be the simplest way for you to create it and what is going to fit in with your lifestyle. If you are very busy, don't try to make everything yourself. Accept help from willing hands, however young they are. Even little ones can hold a paintbrush and sprinkle glitter on glue.

You'll also want to consider what materials you have at hand. If you have lots of red fabric, then perhaps your daughter would like to dress up as Little Red Riding Hood – the cloak is very straightforward. Similarly, it doesn't take long to transform green material into a dinosaur or elf costume. Rather than go out and make a special purchase, you might be able to dye an old sheet or shirt the shade you want. And remember that you can often pick up useful garments and assorted fabric remnants at yard sales and thrift shops (so long as you have got somewhere you can store them without taking up valuable space at home). It's also a good idea to keep a selection of old buttons, metallic wrappers and so on. You'll find many ways you can use these to add interest to an outfit.

Whatever costumes you decide to make, I hope your children enjoy dressing up in them as much as mine have.

Juliet Moxley

SPRINGTIME CREATURES

After a long gray winter why not celebrate the arrival of spring with these brightly colored animal outfits? Just think what fun it will be dressing up as a chick or bunny at Easter. You could have your very own Easter parade at home, where everyone has to make their own special bonnet decorated with paper flowers and ribbons. Later you can have a competition to choose the best one. The winner, of course, gets a chocolate bunny!

MAKING THE COSTUMES

Making a Bunny Tail

1 Place a saucer on the back of white fake fur and, using a crayon, draw around it. Cut out the circle.

2 Using a needle and thread, sew running stitches around the edge of the circle.

3 Tighten the running stitches so that the fur is gathered into a fluffy, round tail shape. Secure by knotting the two ends of the thread together and, using a safety pin, attach the tail to the bunny.

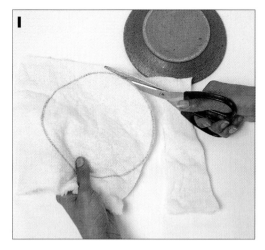

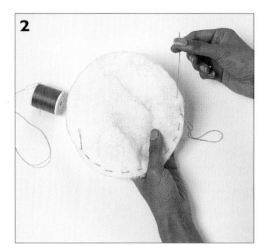

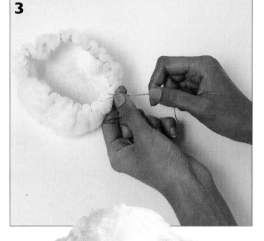

★ For a bunny head, use the hood pattern on page 61 and make it in white fur with long ears attached. The ears are very simple to make: cut two long ear shapes from white fur and two pink felt linings. Stitch the pink felt to the ears and then stitch the ears on either side of the hood.

★ Finish off the bunny outfit by wearing a white T-shirt or sweatshirt and tights.

★ A chicken hood is made from yellow fake fur with a yellow-orange beak attached. The beak is made from two pieces of triangular felt and a piece of interfacing. Wear a yellow T-shirt and tights to complete the outfit.

Other Ideas

★ Make a lamb hood from woolly fake fur, and its tail from a long piece of fake fur. Complete the outfit by wearing a white T-shirt and tights.

★ Make an Easter crown from fake flowers wired together.

★ Make an Easter bonnet by taking an old straw hat and decorating it with different-colored ribbons and paper flowers.

THINGS TO DO

These activities are even more fun if you are dressed up for Easter and have invited friends to a springtime party.

Hunting for eggs

You will need Basket or other container for each child playing the game; selection of small chocolate or sugar-coated eggs – preferably wrapped in shiny paper.

To play Hide all the eggs in the house or garden well before the game is to start. Then give the children various tasks such as, "Find three speckled eggs," or "Find four eggs wrapped in blue paper and three wrapped in silver." This prevents one child from collecting all the hidden eggs and also means that everyone has something to take home.

Animal charades

This is a team game for younger children. It requires three or more players per team. Before the game starts, explain that no sound effects are allowed.

You will need A list of animals for each team. It is a good idea to give the teams different animals so that players can't pick up hints by watching another team.

To play Select a child to go first. Secretly tell him or her which animal to be. He or she then acts out the animal to the rest of the team. Give the team member who correctly guesses the name of the animal another animal for the team to guess. Whichever team finishes the whole list first wins.

Painting eggs

This is a good activity to keep children occupied while they are waiting for guests to arrive at an Easter party.

You will need Hard boiled eggs (so that all the children will have at least one to decorate, plus a few extra); wax crayons (for younger children); wool or string (for older children) and saucepans filled with different-colored dyes. Use red, yellow and blue water.

How to proceed Each child selects an egg to decorate. Younger children should use wax crayons. Encourage them to color their eggs with thick patterns, as this is easier to do. Older children can wind string or wool around the eggs to create a pattern. Then the children dip the eggs in colored water. Once the eggs are dry, cut off the string or wool to reveal the pattern.

CIRCUS CLOWNS

What could be more fun than to be the star of the show, dressed up in a colorful clown outfit? It's easy to adapt existing clothes, perhaps decorating a swimsuit with sequins or using eye-catching suspenders to hold up a pair of baggy trousers. You can add lots of fun and simple-to-make details — for example, gather a piece of brightly colored net to tie around the neckline of the clown costume, or decorate a hat with pom-poms.

MAKING THE COSTUMES

★ Make a clown's costume (see previous page) from an all-in-one pattern (see pages 58–60) made from lots of bright fabrics. Cover it in ribbons, add patch pockets and a ribbon ruff collar.

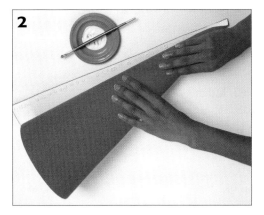

Making a Clown's Hat

1 Using the template on page 62 as a guide, draw the shape of the hat on a piece of colored tagboard and cut it out.

2 Roll the tagboard into a cone shape and secure the edges with glue or double-sided tape.

3 Glue pom-poms around the edge and front of the hat. You can attach a piece of elastic to the sides of the hat which the child can wear under the chin.

Clown Shoes

You can make false shoes for a clown easily and quickly from cardboard. Place a shoe on a large piece of cardboard and draw an enlarged shoe shape around it. Cut out the large shoe shape and also cut a

hole in the center of the cardboard for the foot to fit through. Paint the cardboard whatever color you like – brown, white, black, a mixture – and then draw laces and a shoe tongue and paint on a patch. Make a second shoe and wear them over ordinary shoes. Just don't wear them when its raining!

Other Ideas

★ Paint a clown face using face paints: make a big mouth and rosy cheeks.

★ Why not continue with the circus theme? A ringmaster costume is easy to adapt from an old jacket and top hat. A bow tie will complete the outfit.

★ Be a weight lifter in a bathing suit with a broomstick that has balloons tied on either end.

★ To be an acrobat, wear a leotard decorated with sequins.

★ If you are inviting friends for a circus party, you can decorate paper plates with clown faces to make snack time more special. Simply cut out colored paper for the eyes and mouth. Don't forget to add a bright red nose for each. You could also turn the plate into a clown mask by cutting holes for the eyes to see through and attaching a piece of elastic to hold the plate around the head over the ears.

GAMES TO PLAY
Pass the hats

This game is quite difficult for very young children to play, so I have also included a simplified version that they will be able to manage.

You will need Enough hats so that each child has one to wear; tape recorder with music cassettes.

To play The children wear their hats and stand in a circle facing their right. While the music is playing, the children take the hat off the person in front of them and put it on their own head. They continue doing this until the music stops. Practice this several times so everyone knows what to do; then remove one hat and let the game begin. This time, when the music stops the person left without a hat is out. Each time a person is out, remove another hat from the circle. When only two children are left, they should face each other. The winner is the child left wearing the hat.

An alternative for very young children is to throw the hats into the middle of the circle. The number of hats must be one less than the number of children. When the music stops, the children quickly pick up a hat and put it on. The child without a hat is out. Remove another hat from the pile, and the game continues.

Pass the package - with a difference

This is unlike the traditional game of pass the package and much less messy because it does not involve lots of layers of paper.

You will need Two packages wrapped in the ordinary way – one should be a prize and the other a booby prize; tape recorder with music cassettes.

To play The children sit in a circle on the floor. Hand the packages to two children opposite each other. The packages should be passed in the same direction until the music stops. The children holding the packages are out. This continues until only two players are left. These two pass the packages between them and open the one in their hands when the music stops.

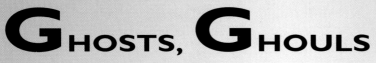

GHOSTS, GHOULS

AND WITCHES

Whether trick-or-treating or running around and going bump in the night, Hallowe'en is the perfect occasion for dressing up and frightening your friends. Hallowe'en costumes are easy to make – try creating a mummy made from toilet paper, a ghost from a sheet and a witch's hat from black tagboard. You can construct from simple cutouts of bats, pumpkins and black cats. Don't forget a witch needs a broom to pretend to ride on.

Making the Costumes

★ **For a witch, make a hat (as described as right) and make a cloak by following the instructions below.**

Making a Witch's Cloak

1 To make a full cloak you will need a large square of black fabric. Fold the square in half and then in half again. Draw a small curve in the folded corner for the neck and a large curve on the outer edge for the hem. Cut along the curves.

2 Open the material. You will have a large circle with a hole in the center. Cut a straight line from the small circle to the edge of the fabric. This will be the front of the cloak. For the collar, see steps 7 and 8 on page 57. Attach a red ribbon to tie the collar of the cloak and neaten the hem with a running stitch.

3 Cut out tissue lamé stars and moons and appliqué them all over the cloak.

1

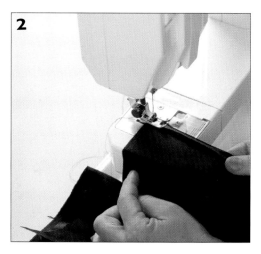

2

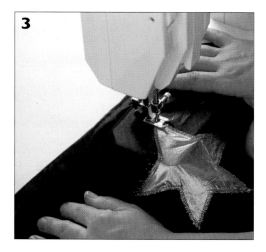

3

Making Witches' hats

Witches' hats are fun to make. Draw around a large dinner plate onto a piece of black tagboard. Cut out the circle and then cut it in half – each half makes one hat. Take one half and roll into a cone, gluing the two edges together. To make the brim, measure the circumference of the cone and cut out another circle with the circumference 2in (5cm) wider. Draw a circle 3in (7.5cm) in from the edge and cut along this line. Discard the inner circle. You are left with a hoop. At even intervals along this hoop, make 1in (2.5cm) cuts. Bend back at right angles and tape them to the inside of the hat. Finish off each hat by gluing on gold and silver stars.

Making a Hallowe'en Mask

You can help children make their own Hallowe'en mask. You need brown paper bags or paper plates, empty yogurt cups containing glue, frozen treat sticks or brushes to apply the glue, aluminum foil, lengths of wool in various colors, thick wax crayons, scissors, string, colored straws, gold and silver stars and gold and silver felt-tipped pens.

Help the child make holes for eyes and mouth in the paper bag or plate and then let the child decorate the mask in any way he chooses, using the materials provided. The child can add hair by gluing lengths of wool to the bag or plate above the eyes or down the sides.

Children can wear paper bags over their head and hold up plates in front of their face or secure them around the back of their head with a piece of elastic.

Other Ideas

★ Make a ghost from an old sheet with two eye holes cut out and circled with black paint.
★ Create a skeleton using a black T-shirt and tights with bones made from crêpe paper sewn or glued on.
★ Make a severed hand from an old rubber glove with bits of cereal (warts) and hair stuck on. Paint the whole thing green – it is truly revolting!
★ Add a pair of devil's horns by molding two pieces of red plastic wrap onto pipe cleaners and then twisting the pipe cleaners onto a headband.
★ Be a cobweb by wearing elastic over a leotard and tights. Add a plastic spider to be even more frightening.

INTO OUTER SPACE

From the man in the moon to astronauts and aliens, the idea of rockets, stars and galaxies always grabs the imagination of children. Bicycle or crash helmets make convincing space helmets, and you can spray boots silver. Try gluing tinfoil on tagboard to make a spacesuit. You can make props from recycled tinfoil dishes and bottle tops.

MAKING THE COSTUMES

★ For a spaceman (see photograph on previous page), wear a tabard (see page 57) in gray or metallic fabric over white or silver tights and a T-shirt.

★ Make an alien (see photograph on previous page) by covering a balloon with papier-mâché, gluing on bits of an egg carton and cutting out a hole for the head. Spray the whole thing in silver.

Robot man

A robot made from cardboard boxes is a really effective space companion. Use a large box for the body. Attach a smaller one for the head and even smaller ones for the arms, legs and feet – shoe boxes are ideal for the feet. Decorate by spraying with silver or covering with tinfoil and sticking on old tin cans, bits of tubing, wheels, etc. To dress up as a robot, wear a decorated box round your middle, leaving holes for your arms, legs and neck.

Spray painting instructions

1 To decorate anything with a galaxy theme, draw a star on newspaper and cut it out with scissors to make a stencil.

2 Cover your work surface with paper to prevent it from becoming covered with paint. Hold the stencil firmly onto whatever you are decorating and spray with silver paint.

3 To give a golden aura to planets, make a stencil the same way but use gold paint. Always lift the stencil up carefully when you have finished spraying.

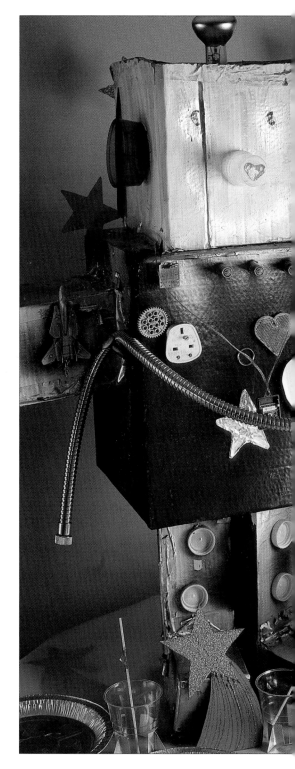

Other Ideas

★ Make a backpack from a cardboard box covered in tinfoil attached with elastic shoulder straps.

★ For a robot, wear a tabard (see page 57) in metallic fabric with tinsel, bits of tubing and bottle tops glued or sewn on. Spray a brown paper bag with silver paint and cut out holes for the eyes and mouth. Wear boots sprayed with silver paint as space boots.

★ Wear a motorcycle helmet.

★ For the man in the moon, cut out a cardboard crescent moon and paint it silver. Attach it with straps to the chest and wear with gray tights and a sweater beneath.

★ Make a star costume from a star-shaped piece of cardboard sprayed with silver and lengths of tinsel stuck all around the edges.

★ For a star headdress, use a headband bent into a star shape and wrapped in tinsel.

GAMES TO PLAY

Here are a few games that children aged seven or eight and above will enjoy while dressed as spacemen and astronauts.

Planet plodding

You will need Two inflated balloons, each attached to 2 ft (60cm) lengths of string for each child playing the game.

To play Tie a balloon to each child's ankles and let them practice walking around for a short while (taking care not to burst the balloons). Once the game starts, the idea is to pretend to be walking around testing the planet's surface and to burst the balloons belonging to any other space explorers by treading or jumping on them. Once both his balloons are burst, the child is out. The winner is the last person to have one or two balloons left.

Noises from outer space

This is a quiet game to play either among individuals or between teams.

You will need Various objects with which to make sounds, like shutting a book, jangling keys, lighting a match, cutting paper with scissors; pencils and paper for the players to write their answers on.

To play The organizer making the noises hides out of sight with the props and says, "Sound number one", while making the noise. Give the children enough time to write down what they think the answer is before making the next sound. The winner is the person who identifies the most noises correctly.

GARDEN DWELLERS

Why not combine dressing up as a scarecrow, snail or flower with a feast? Plan to have a picnic outside in the garden, but if the sun refuses to come out, you can always move it indoors. You can even have indoor grass.

MAKING THE COSTUMES

★ Turn yourself into a scarecrow with a mop head. For hair, stick straw or raffia under an old and battered straw hat.

★ Borrow old and tattered jeans or corduroys and wear with old misshapen sweaters or shirts with rips or buttons missing.

★ To make the outfit authentic, put a wooden spoon (stick end outward) down your sleeves, with a few bits of straw sticking out.

★ Complete the outfit with an old pair of boots or shoes.

★ Make a snail by wearing gray tights and sweater. Attach a round, gray paper lampshade on the back, held on by gray straps. Tie a long padded tail ending in a point to the waist. For the antennae, attach some pipe cleaners, with pom-poms wired to the ends, to a hairband.

Other Ideas

★ Create a bee costume by dressing in bright yellow tights and a yellow T-shirt painted with black stripes using a fabric pen. Make some antennae with yellow and black pipe cleaners and pom-poms.

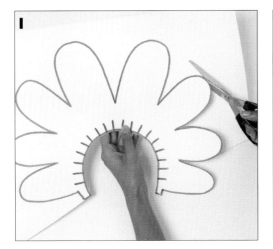

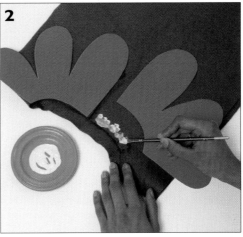

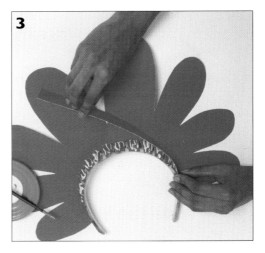

Making a Flower Costume

1 Make a green felt tabard (see instructions on page 57). To make the petal collar for the tabard, use tagboard and follow the template on page 63. Draw on the petals as shown. Cut out and glue to the front neckline of the tabard.

2 Use tagboard to make a petal headpiece. Use the headpiece template on page 63 as a guide. When you cut out the semicircle on the headpiece, cut little incisions as shown. These will act as tabs which will make it easier to glue the petal headpiece onto a child's headband.

3 Fold out the tabs, apply glue to the headpiece and press the tabs firmly down on the headband. Glue down a long strip of tagboard or material over the headband to hide the glue and the tabs.

A GAME TO PLAY
Musical statues or trees

Children of all ages enjoy this. It can be played both inside and out.

You will need Tape machine with music cassettes.

To play Everyone dances or runs around while the music is playing. If the game is being played inside, when the music stops all the children must stand as still as possible, pretending to be statues. Anyone who moves is out. If this is being played outside and there are one or two trees not too far away, the children should run to the nearest tree when the music stops. The last child to reach the safety of a tree is out. This continues until there is just one child left – the winner!

FAIRIES AND ELVES

Young children love
fairyland. It's where dreams
are made and wishes
fulfilled. You can have lots
of fun making costumes
from things around the
house. If it's Christmas, you
could pretend to be one of
Santa's elves or the fairy
from the top of the tree.
Add a magical sparkle to
your fairy dress with tinsel,
glitter and silver spray.

MAKING THE COSTUMES

★ **For a fairy, decorate a leotard with a crinoline skirt and sequins.**
★ **Decorate a full-length petticoat with a frilly nylon skirt with glitter.**

Fairy Wings

Make fairy wings from silver tagboard or cardboard edged with Christmas tinsel and attach them with two elastic straps to wear over the shoulders. Alternatively, create an effective pair of translucent fairy wings by bending wire coat hangers into wing shapes and gluing netting over them.

A Magic Wand

Make a wand from a dowel sprayed with silver and two star-shaped pieces of cardboard covered in glitter or painted silver.

Pixie

★ For a pixie or elf outfit, use a tabard of green felt (see page 57) with a zigzag hem with bells attached. Wear it with green or black tights and pixie boots and make a pointed green hat with a bell sewn onto the end.
★ Make false ears from papier-mâché (see page 56), sewn or stuck onto the sides of the elf's cap.

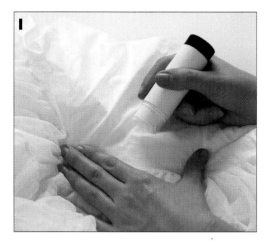

To Decorate a Fairy Dress

1 Attach a net petticoat to a T-shirt or leotard – white or pastel colors are best for a fairy dress. Spread fabric glue evenly along the hem of the petticoat.

2 Cover the work area with paper, and then sprinkle silver glitter onto the glued area; shake off the excess glitter. Fill any gaps by resticking and sprinkling on more glitter.

3 Sew or glue silver sequins to the bodice and shoulder straps and around the neckline of the T-shirt or leotard.

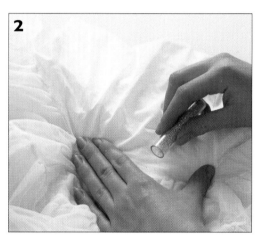

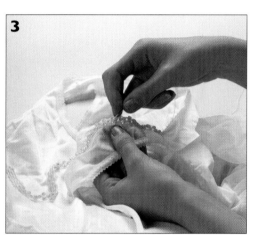

GAMES TO PLAY

What can it be?

You will need Two prizes loosely wrapped in five or six layers of paper with string and tape.

To play The children take turns trying to guess what is inside the packages. Each feels a package and asks a question which will help discover what is inside. Every time a child asks something that proves useful in this quest, remove one layer of wrapping. This continues until the last layer is removed. The player who asked is then allowed to keep the prize. The number of layers depends on the ages of the children and how long you want the game to last.

Puff ball

You will need One table tennis ball per team; one large straw per player; tape to act as a finishing line.

To play Divide the players into teams and line them up at one end of the room. Put the tape on the floor at the other end of the room to mark the finish. The first person on each team puts the ball on the floor and at the command "Go" blows the ball using the straw until it has crossed the finishing line. Then he picks up the ball, runs back to the team and gives it to the next person, who repeats the exercise. The first team to have all players complete this wins.

COWBOYS AND INDIANS

It's great fun to dress up as cowboys and Indians. You can be an Indian chief, cowgirl or even the Lone Ranger complete with mask and wooden hobbyhorse. To become a cowboy, decorate old flannel shirts or jeans with fringing. Bandannas around the neck and a sheriff's star all help to create a Wild West look.

MAKING THE COSTUMES

★ **Make a chief's headdress using feathers from a duster sewn onto brown fabric as described to the right.**
★ **Make a squaw's dress as described below.**
★ **Use face paints in bright yellows and reds to decorate the squaws' and braves' faces.**
★ **For a cowboy shirt, use an old flannel shirt and perhaps add fringing on the pockets.**
★ **Wear an old denim jacket.**
★ **Buy cowboy hats cheaply at a toy stores or bend an old hat into shape.**

Cowboy Trousers

Add fringing to a pair of old jeans to make cowboy trousers. Measure the outside leg of the trousers from the waist to the hem. Double this measurement to figure out how much you need. Look for fringing in fabric stores; lampshade fringing is ideal. Cut the fringe in half and attach it down the outside seam of the jeans using double-sided tape. Alternatively, sew the fringing on by hand using a running stitch.

Squaw's dress

You can make a squaw's dress (right) from a brown tabard (see page 57) of cotton, suede or similar fabric. Sew up the sides leaving room for the arms. Cut from the bottom of the skirt up 8in (20cm) at intervals of 1in (2.5cm) to make

fringing. Cut a slit 6in (15cm) in the front of the neck. Cut holes and thread them with a brown shoe-lace. Decorate the neckline with beads or feathers. Add bunches of different-colored feathers cut from a feather duster and sew all over the costume. Add colored buttons to the places where you have sewn on the feathers.

Indian Chief Headdress

1 Cut a piece of brown fabric long enough to tie around the head and extend down the sides of the body. Taper the ends. Glue on circles of felt.

2 Remove feathers from brightly colored feather dusters.

3 Sew the feathers in place using a zigzag stitch.

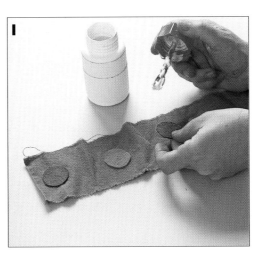

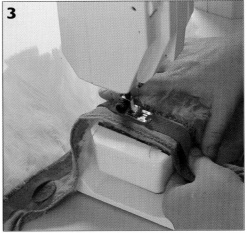

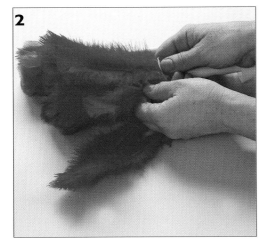

PLAYING COWBOYS AND INDIANS

This is a fun game to play when lots of children are dressed up as cowboys and Indians.

You will need Lengths of rope or thick string.

To play Divide the children into two teams – one of "cowboys" and the other "Indians." One team member stands separately while the others get into pairs and stand or sit back to back. Each pair should be tied together with several knots. When you shout, "Go," the spare team member has to untie all the knots and free all the captives in his or her team. The first team to have all its members untied is the winner. If the numbers are uneven and one child has not had a turn, it is best to play the whole game again. If the game is being played outside, children could be tied to trees or garden furniture instead of each other. Once free, team members can make appropriate noises (whooping and warbling) to encourage the cowboy or Indian doing the untying and to add to the excitement.

Other Ideas

★ Decorate jeans with fringing down the side.

★ Make a poncho by cutting a hole in the center of an old blanket or wrap.

★ For a sheriff's badge, cut out a cardboard star and paint it silver. Glue a pin on the back to attach.

MYSTERIOUS MERMAID

Make a splash with this shimmering mermaid costume. Use metallic fabrics and netting in the blue and green colors of the sea to create a long fish tail and headdress. Use shells collected from the sea-shore to make a suitable mermaid's necklace or bracelet. Other fun seaside costumes include a diver, Neptune, or even a sand castle!

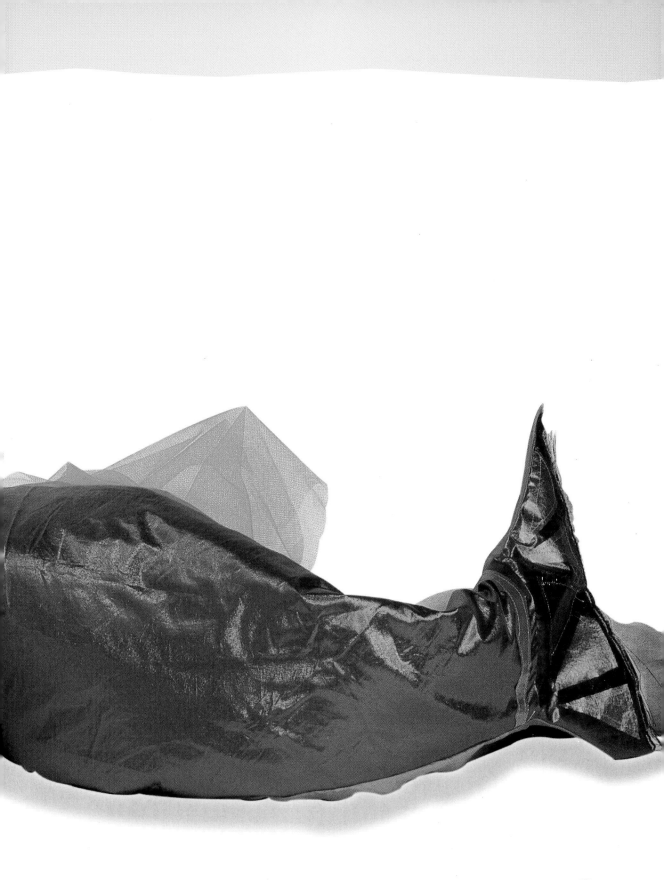

MAKING THE COSTUME

★ **Create a mermaid's costume from a plain pink bathing suit wrapped around with netting to which a padded and appliquéd fish tail is attached (see step-by-step instructions below).**

★ **Attach shells onto blue lamé fabric as a headband.**

Making a Mermaid's Tail

1 Draw a tail (see page 62) the length of the wearer from waist to toe and then cut out the shape twice from metallic fabric and once from a length of wadding. Sew some scales in shiny, metallic fabric onto the tip of the tail.

2 Place the two metallic tail pieces together with shiny sides facing in. Sew down both sides and around the tail. Leave the top open.

3 Turn the material the right way around and insert the wadding. Pin a long length of blue netting to the front of the mermaid's tail. It should be long enough to tie around the waist. Finish off the tail by sewing the top shut.

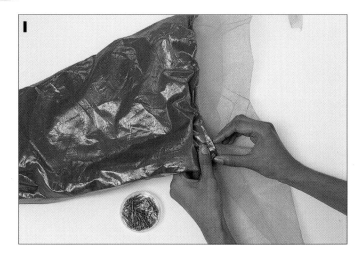

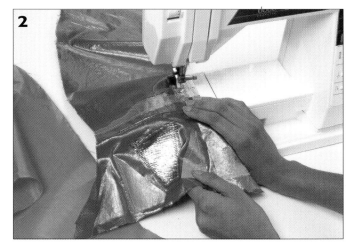

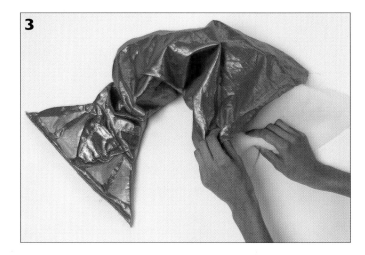

A Mermaid's Necklace

Finish off the mermaid outfit by adding a necklace or bracelet. Paint small pieces of macaroni blue and green and, once dry, thread them onto some cotton and tie around the neck or wrist. Alternatively, glue some seashells to a length of cotton, spray them gold and tie around the neck.

Other ideas

★ For Neptune, make a tabard (see page 57) from tissue lamé in silver, blue or green tied with seaweed or a belt made from shells.

★ Make his trident from a piece of cardboard and attach·it to a dowel sprayed with silver.

★ Cut fish-shaped masks from cardboard and paint them with tropical fish colors and patterns.

★ To be a diver, wear a snorkel, face mask and a rubber suit or black leotard.

★ Be a sand castle made from corrugated cardboard with shells and a beached starfish glued or drawn on. Alternatively, you can make a big sand castle to hide in.

GAMES TO PLAY

Musical islands

This is a great game to play at a party with a seaside theme and is a variation on musical chairs. Two advantages are that you don't need lots of room to accommodate the chairs and also children can help to make the props in advance.

You will need Islands drawn or painted on paper (one for each child playing the game); tape recorder with music cassettes.

To play Place the islands on the sea (the floor). When the music plays, the children must move around in the water. As soon as the music stops, they have to run and hop onto an island. When the music starts up again, take away an island while the children are moving around. This time, when the music stops the child who does not land on an island is out. Continue in this way until there are only two children and one island left in the game. This time, when the music stops the first child to step onto the island is the winner. To make the game more complicated, tell the children to stand on one leg when they are on the islands. If they fall into the sea, they are also out of the game.

Squeal mermaid squeal

This is a variation on the old traditional game "Squeak piggy squeak", which younger children find very amusing.

You will need A cushion and a scarf to be used as a blindfold.

To play Ask for a volunteer to be blindfolded. Once you have checked that the child cannot see, turn him or her around three times. The rest of the children then find a seat in the room (or sit on chairs in a circle around the blindfolded person) and keep very quiet. The blindfolded player is then handed a cushion and moves around until he or she finds someone and puts the cushion on their lap. He or she then sits on the cushion and says, "Squeal mermaid squeal", and must then wait for the player underneath to respond. The blindfolded child has to guess on whose lap he or she is sitting. If the guess is correct, these two then swap places, and if wrong the blindfolded player continues and has another turn.

KNIGHTS AND DAMSELS

Why not have a fantasy adventure, with beautiful jewelled costumes and crowns and tiaras? It's a chance to play a beautiful princess or a gallant knight, or to be a page boy or a damsel in distress.

MAKING THE COSTUMES

★ A damsel (see previous page) can wear a pointed conical hat as described opposite.
★ For the damsel's top, crisscross the front of a T-shirt with ribbons and add a sequin at each intersection.
★ Make a knight's shield and helmet as described opposite.
★ For a cape, use gold fabric and add a drawstring 2in (5cm) from the top to make a stand-up collar.
★ A glittery crown adds some glamour – see the description below.

Making a Glitter Crown

1 Cut a crown shape out of cardboard. Stick lumps of wet tissue over the cardboard and then cover with layers of papier-mâché (see page 56).

2 Paint with white latex paint. Smooth out metallic candy wrappers until they are flat and then stick them onto the lumps on the crown.

3 Paint the crown gold and then stick decorations all over it. Add patterns in silver pen. Thread elastic at the back to hold it on the head.

A Knight's Helmet

A helmet is easy to make out of papier-mâché (see page 56), built up over a balloon. Blow up a balloon and then cover it with five or six layers of papier-mâché. When the papier-mâché is dry, pop the balloon and cut away the front of the helmet to accommodate the face. Add a yogurt cup upside down to the top of the helmet. Cover the whole thing with another coat of papier-mâché, paint it silver and add a feather to the top.

A Damsel's Hat

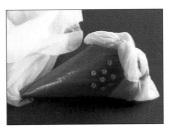

Cut a conical hat from tagboard, as if making a witch's hat (see page 19), but before folding the hat into a cone shape, glue on a metallic fabric or spray with gold or silver. Cut a strip of net or a fine fabric and gather it round the bottom in swags and stick sequins on the front of the hat. Make a hole about the size of a table tennis ball at the top, cut a long piece of netting and poke it into the top, letting the rest flow down to the floor.

A Knight's Shield

A shield can be made from a large laundry detergent box. Draw an oval, round or heart-shaped outline on the back of the box and cut it out. Cut the top with the handle off the box and stick this on the back of the shield. To decorate the shield, spray it with silver or cover in foil and then paint it with poster paints. You may wish to make up your own coat of arms or paint on the wearer's initials.

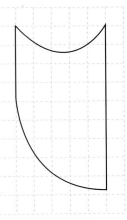

FUN IN THE JUNGLE

Here's an opportunity to dress up as wild beasts of the jungle! Or you can make jungle costumes from animal print fabrics worn over bathing suits with flower garlands. To add to the jungle atmosphere, why not make some green crepe-paper creepers and large tissue-paper butterflies and flowers? You can make trees from cardboard tubes painted green with large green paper leaves stuck on.

MAKING THE COSTUMES

★ **Make tiger and leopard print costumes using the all-in-one pattern on pages 58–60 and the hood pattern featured on page 61.**

Other Ideas

★ Make a monkey tail from fake fur and fabric and then stitch to a leotard.
★ For a parrot costume, wear brightly colored tights and a T-shirt. You can add a green hood with an orange beak to give a truly authentic look – just follow the instructions on page 61.
★ To complete the parrot, make paper wings and paint in bright colors.

If you are having a jungle costume party, decorate the room with paper trees and butterflies.

Butterfly

★ **For a butterfly costume, wear a black leotard and tights.**
★ **Make wings from a sheet of fabric decorated with fabric paints or appliqué. Attach to the leotard at the shoulders, and baste down the middle of the back.**

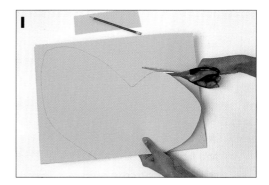

Making a Pair of Wings

1 Fold a sheet of colored tagboard in half and using the template on page 63 as a guide, draw the butterfly wings, making sure the straight edge of each wing lies on the fold in the card. Cut out the wings, and don't forget to cut out the tab as well. Open out the wings.

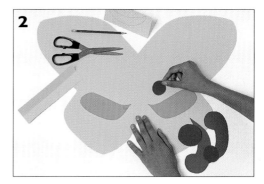

2 Cut out various shapes from brightly colored paper. Glue them onto the front and back of the wings.

3 Using tape, secure the tab along the crease in the center of the wings, leaving the top and the bottom ends open. Use these openings to thread two lengths of black elastic through the tube created by the tab. Tie the ends of the elastic together to form loops for the child's arms to go through.

A GAME TO PLAY

Animal search

This is an alternative to the popular game of hunt the thimble and is a real treat for younger children who have dressed up as animals and are pretending to be in a jungle.

You will need Six or more animal shapes cut out of plain colored paper – enough different species for each child who is going to play the game. The shapes should be obvious to identify (like elephants, monkeys and lions), so if you run out of easy shapes, cut out birds, butterflies,

snakes, tortoises or whatever as well). Hide all the paper shapes around the house. If there are any rooms that are out of bounds, close the door and put up a notice saying, "Keep Out", or tell the children which rooms they are allowed to search.

To play You can either tell the children to find one of each animal, or tell them to find all the shapes of one particular animal. The winner is the first person to find all the shapes they have been asked to look for.

47

NURSERY RHYMES

Here is a great opportunity to be your favorite nursery rhyme character. You can be Goldilocks or one of the three bears, Little Red Riding Hood or the Big Bad Wolf. Simple masks and props will allow you to be anything you want to be!

MAKING THE COSTUMES

★ Make a teddy bear hood out of fake fur using the pattern on page 61.
★ Use the all-in-one pattern on pages 58–60 to make the body of the teddy bear.
★ For a simpler costume, attach round ears made from fake fur lined in pink felt to a headband and blacken your nose.
★ Wear brown woolen mittens for paws.
★ Make a teddy bear mask from cardboard covered in felt.

Making Little Red Riding Hood's Cloak

1 For the cloak, follow the instructions on page 57. For the hood, cut a smaller circle of red fabric and cut that in half. Sew the two halves together along the straight edge of the semicircle.

2 Insert a piece of boning along that seam – this will make the hood stand out around the face.

3 Gather the two sections of material from the semicircle and sew them onto the neckline of the cloak. Sew over the raw edges on the front and hem of the cloak to neaten up. Add red ribbon ties at the neck.

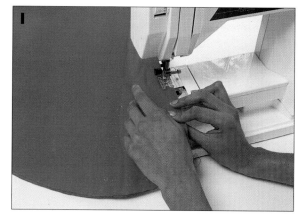

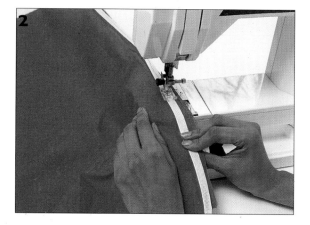

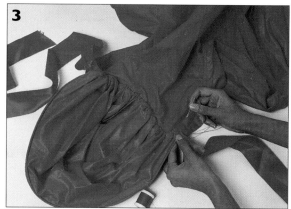

Other Ideas

★ You can make a fierce wolf mask from cardboard covered in gray felt.
★ Little Red Riding Hood's dress can simply be a pretty party dress with frills.
★ To dress up as Little Miss Muffet, wear a mobcap; a fancy cap that ties under the chin, made from a 30in (75cm) circle of fabric with elastic inserted 4in (10cm) from the outside edge to make a frill. To complete the outfit, carry a bowl and spoon for curds and whey, and a plastic spider.
★ Simple Simon's pie man only needs to wear a chef's apron and carry a tray of pies.

Making a Pig Mask

1 Hold a paper plate up to your face and mark the position of your eyes, nose and mouth with a pencil. Cut out the eye holes. Attach a length of black elastic.

2 To make a nose, squash a small paper cup and glue it on the plate. Paint the plate and the nose pink and add a pink mouth with a felt pen.

3 Cut out pink felt ears and attach to the back of the mask.

4 The finished mask.

GAMES TO PLAY

Younger children enjoy pretending to be nursery rhyme characters and playing games on this theme.

Nursery rhyme charades

To play Everyone sits in a circle and you ask if any-one would like to act out a nursery rhyme for the others to guess. You have to explain that no talking is allowed and everyone has got to pretend. Some children will find it easy to think of a suitable rhyme but younger children may need you to whisper a suggestion to them such as "Humpty Dumpty." In this case, you whisper to the child that he or she should go into the middle of the circle and pretend to sit on an imaginary wall and then fall off. Tell them to do their mime again until one of the others guesses correctly and it becomes their turn.
Here are some other suggestions:
Little Miss Muffet would sit on an imaginary chair pretending to eat from a bowl and then look frightened and run away from an imaginary spider. Jack Horner is easy to act out: sitting in a corner, putting a thumb in a pretend pie, and then pulling out his thumb and looking smug and smiling. Award prizes for each successful act.

Ring-a-round the rosey

Even shy children who are very young will be happy to join in this game to break the tension at the beginning of a party.
To play All the children hold hands and walk or skip around in a circle while singing the nursery rhyme "Ring around the rosey." If you want to make it into more of a game, when it comes to the traditional "All fall down" part of the song, the last child to fall down is out. This continues until only one child left and this child is declared the winner and given a prize.

Dinosaur

Create your very own Jurassic Park or Land That Time Forgot by dressing up as a caveman or dinosaur. To make the costumes, use scraps of fake fur or brown fabric and, for dinosaur masks, use cardboard and egg cartons. You could also design your very own caveman drawings on the walls of your cave!

MAKING THE COSTUMES

★ Sew together bits of fake fur, suede, or leather scraps using zigzag stitching to make male or female cave costumes.

★ Make a club by following the instructions opposite.

★ Make a dinosaur body from a long length of green fabric, gathered at the neck with elastic. Cut armholes so the dinosaur can use his hands!

★ Make a pterodactyl hood by using the pattern on page 61 and attach felt spikes along the top.

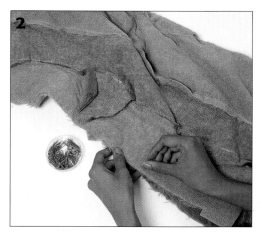

Making a Caveman's Costume

1 Gather together scraps of fake fur, suede and leather. Cut the scraps into long strips, then using a sewing machine, zigzag-stitch these pieces together until you have a rectangular "skin" which is large enough to wrap around a child's body.

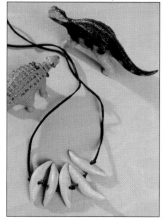

2 Fold this piece in half and then sew the ends together, so you are left with a large tube which the child can slip over his or her head.

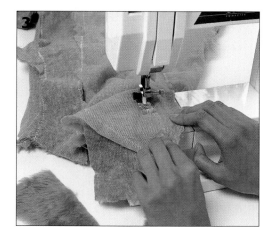

3 Add two straps or cut armholes in the tube.

★ A necklace that looks like real dinosaur teeth (left) will add the finishing touch to a cave costume. Make a tooth necklace by shaping teeth in papier-mâché (see page 56) and stringing them together on a piece of string or a leather shoelace.

You can make a club simply by rolling a large sheet of newspaper into a tube, halving it and sticking the two pieces together with masking tape to make a handle. Blow up a small balloon and cover it with three layers of papier-mâché (see page 56). When the papier-mâché is dry, pop the balloon, cut a hole in the side of the head of the club and insert the handle. Fasten securely in place with masking tape and add another layer of papier-mâché over the top of the whole thing. Decorate the club with brown paint and then apply a coat of clear varnish.

Make Your Own Cave

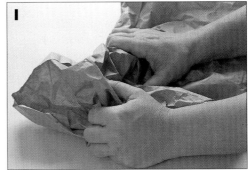

1 Crumple brown paper to give the natural uneven look of caves and stick inside a large box which has been placed on its side.

2 Sponge brown and orangish brown paints over the cave "walls."

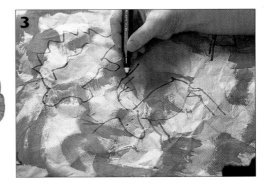

3 The cave is ready for decorating by the cavemen! Using fine black felt pens, draw stick men with spears on the brown wrapping paper.

Papier-Mâché

Papier-mâché is the ideal substance for making models, costumes and props. You can place it over a balloon, on chicken wire, onto cardboard and plastic containers, or mold it into simple shapes. Papier-mâché is very simple to decorate and a final coat of varnish ensures that it will last.

Papier-mâché is basically paper and glue. For all the props in this book I have used newspaper and wallpaper paste. You can also use a flour and water paste.

To make flour and water paste, you need 1 mug of water and 3 mugs of flour. In a saucepan, mix a little of the water with the flour until you have a smooth paste and then add the rest of the water slowly, stirring all the time. Heat the mixture until it boils and let it simmer until the paste thickens. Turn the heat off and use when cold.

To papier-mâché

1 Rip newspapers into strips about 1in (2.5cm) wide. Dip the paper into glue or paste and then squeeze off the excess between thumb and forefinger.

2 Apply the paper strips onto the base you are using. Work one layer at a time and allow to dry between layers. Five or six layers are usually enough for any project.

3 When dry, paint with a coat of white latex paint before decorating.

Costumes

You can make most costumes you are ever likely to need from three basic patterns. You can use a tabard for a red Indian dress, a Peter Pan, elf or pixie, a soldier, or even a painting smock. A cloak can be used by a wizard, a witch, a knight, a lady, Little Red Riding Hood and a conjuror. An all-in-one may be an animal, a racing driver, a clown or a spaceman.

To make a jacket or pants use the top or bottom of the all-in-one pattern and add a generous seam allowance at the waist or hem to allow for alterations.

For a skirt, make a tube of material with an elasticated top which can be adjusted to the size of the wearer.

Cloak

For a photographic step-by-step sequence see page 18.
1 To make a full cloak you will need a large square of fabric measuring 54in x 54in (135cm x 135cm). Fold the square in half and place against the child's shoulder; this will show how long the cloak will be. Open up the material.

2 Fold the square in half and half again.

3 Draw a small curve on the corner with the folds for the neck and a large curve on the opposite corner for the hem.

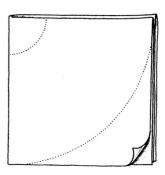

4 Cut along the curves.

5 Open up the material. You will have a large circle with a hole in the center. Cut a straight line from the small circle to the large one. This is the front of the cloak.

6 Fold over ¹/₄in (6mm) of the raw edges and hem to neaten. Add ribbon ties at the neck.

7 If you wish to add a collar, measure the length of the neck and cut a piece of fabric this length (plus ¹/₂in [12mm] seam allowances) by double the depth you wish the collar to be. Fold the collar in half lengthways, right sides facing, and stitch along the narrow ends.

8 Sew the collar onto the neck along one long side, right sides together. Fold the collar down and hand-stitch the other long side onto the neck, hiding any raw edges.

9 To make a hood, cut a smaller circle (27in [68cm]) of fabric and cut in half. With right sides facing, sew the two halves together down their straight edge. Sew a piece of boning along the inside of the seam. This will make the hood stand out around the face. Stitch together and gather the double thickness of the semicircle and sew it onto the neckline.

Simple Cloak

Instead of using a circle, this method uses a rectangle of fabric. Make a channel along one of the narrow ends for the elastic or drawstring.

Neaten the bottom and sides with a hem or running stitch. Fasten the cloak with a button or drawstring. For a knight, appliqué a shield on the back.

Tabard

1 To calculate the amount of fabric needed, measure from the shoulder to the knee, add 2in (5cm) for seam allowance and double the measurement.

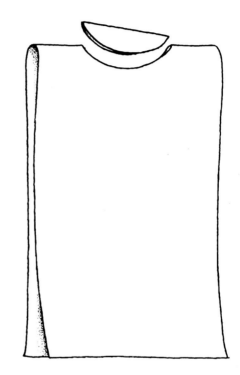

2 Cut your length of fabric, fold it in half and cut a hole large enough to fit over the child's head. If you wish, cut a further slit down the front of about 4in (10cm) and make holes on either side of the slit for lacing.

3 Neaten around the neck and the sides of the tabard. You can sew up the sides if you wish, but leave lots of room for the arms to move easily. Cut a fringe for an Indian dress and a zigzag pattern for a pixie. Decorate according to the costume you are making.

4 If you are not sewing up the sides, sew on ribbon or bias binding tape ties at the sides.

BASIC PATTERNS

All-in-one

From this pattern you can make every conceivable kind of animal as well as a clown and a spaceman.

The pattern fits a 4- to 6-year-old but you can enlarge it by lengthening the body section. Each piece incorporates a $^5/_8$in (15mm) seam allowance.

1 Enlarge the pattern given here onto dressmakers' grid paper or photocopy it. Check that the arms and legs fit your child.

2 Cut out two fronts, two backs, and two sleeves (see page 60) for each costume.

3 With right sides facing, sew the two fronts together as far as the dot.

4 Sew in poppers, Velcro or a zipper down the rest of the front seam.

5 With right sides facing, sew the two backs together down the center back seam. If making an animal, leave a gap for the tail.

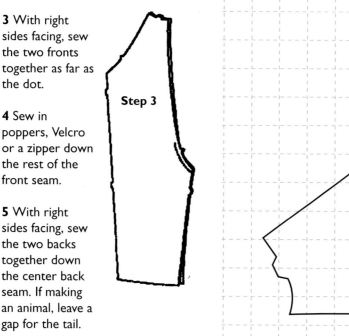

Step 3

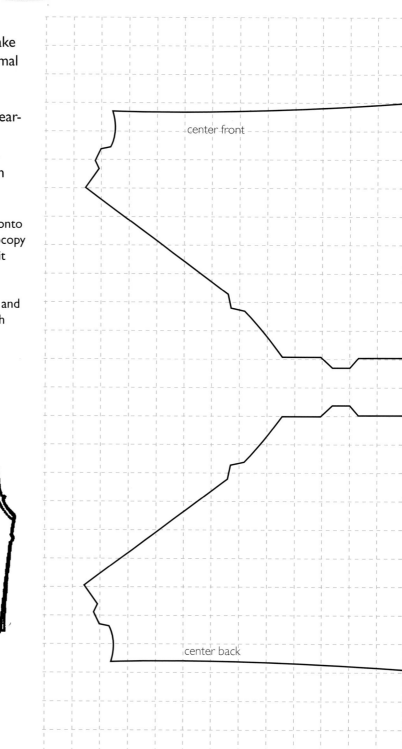

center front

center back

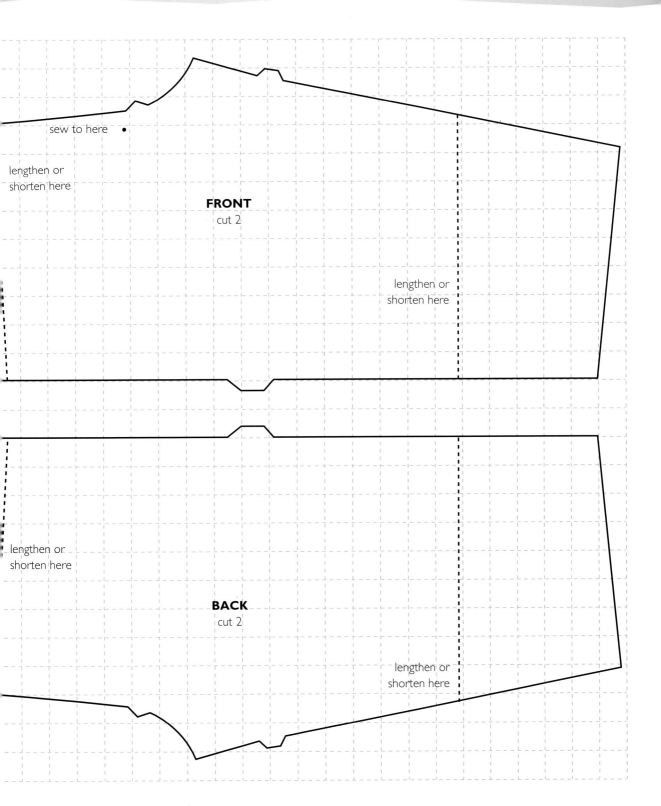

sew to here •

lengthen or
shorten here

FRONT
cut 2

lengthen or
shorten here

lengthen or
shorten here

BACK
cut 2

lengthen or
shorten here

BASIC PATTERNS

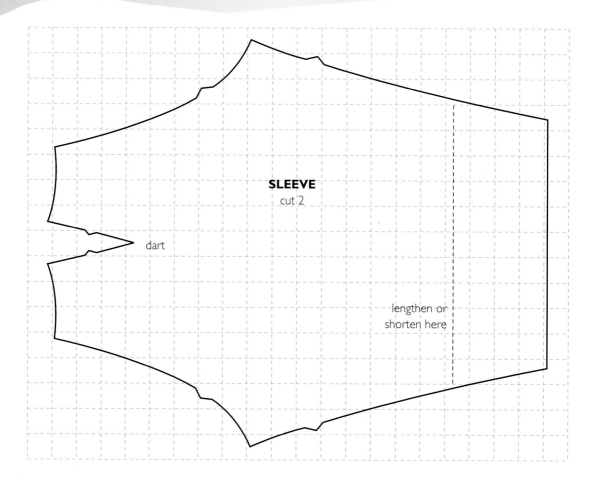

SLEEVE
cut 2

dart

lengthen or
shorten here

6 Sew the darts on the shoulder seams. Pin the sleeves to the edges of the armholes front and back. Sew into position.

7 Sew down all the seams. For a spaceman, add metallic cuffs and complete the outfit with an aluminum foil backpack and crash helmet. For a clown, cut the pattern in different colored and patterned materials. Add patch pockets and a ruff collar.

Step 6

Step 7

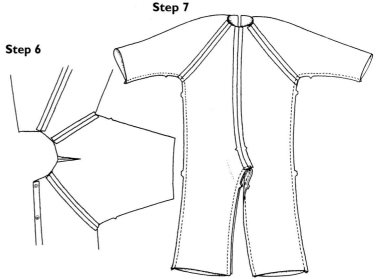

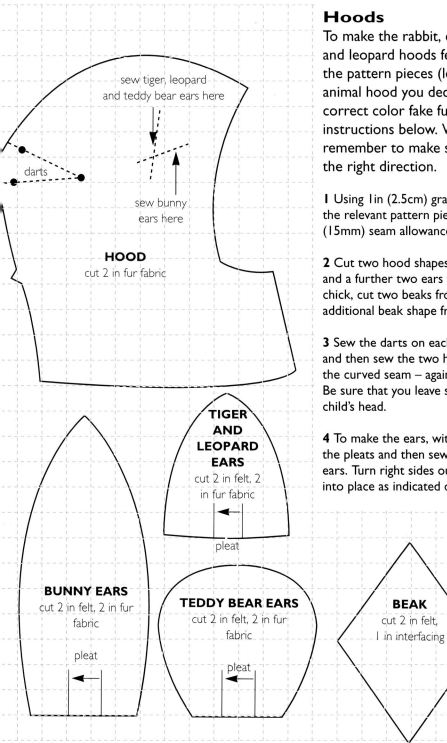

sew tiger, leopard
and teddy bear ears here

darts

sew bunny
ears here

HOOD
cut 2 in fur fabric

**TIGER
AND
LEOPARD
EARS**
cut 2 in felt, 2
in fur fabric

pleat

BUNNY EARS
cut 2 in felt, 2 in fur
fabric

pleat

TEDDY BEAR EARS
cut 2 in felt, 2 in fur
fabric

pleat

BEAK
cut 2 in felt,
1 in interfacing

Hoods

To make the rabbit, chick, teddy bear, tiger and leopard hoods featured in this book, use the pattern pieces (left and below). Whichever animal hood you decide to make, choose the correct color fake fur and then follow the instructions below. When cutting fur fabric, remember to make sure the pile is all going in the right direction.

1 Using 1in (2.5cm) graph paper, draw and cut out the relevant pattern pieces. Each piece has a ⅝in (15mm) seam allowance included in the outline.

2 Cut two hood shapes from fur, two ears from fur and a further two ears from lining fabric or felt. For a chick, cut two beaks from orange felt and an additional beak shape from interfacing.

3 Sew the darts on each piece, right sides together, and then sew the two head pieces together around the curved seam – again, with right sides together. Be sure that you leave space to fit the hood over the child's head.

4 To make the ears, with right sides together stitch the pleats and then sew the felt linings to the fur ears. Turn right sides out and then stitch the ears into place as indicated on the pattern

5 For the chick, iron the interfacing onto one side of one of the beaks and then sew the beaks together with the interfacing sandwiched between them. Sew the beak into place as in the photograph on page 9.

Basic Patterns

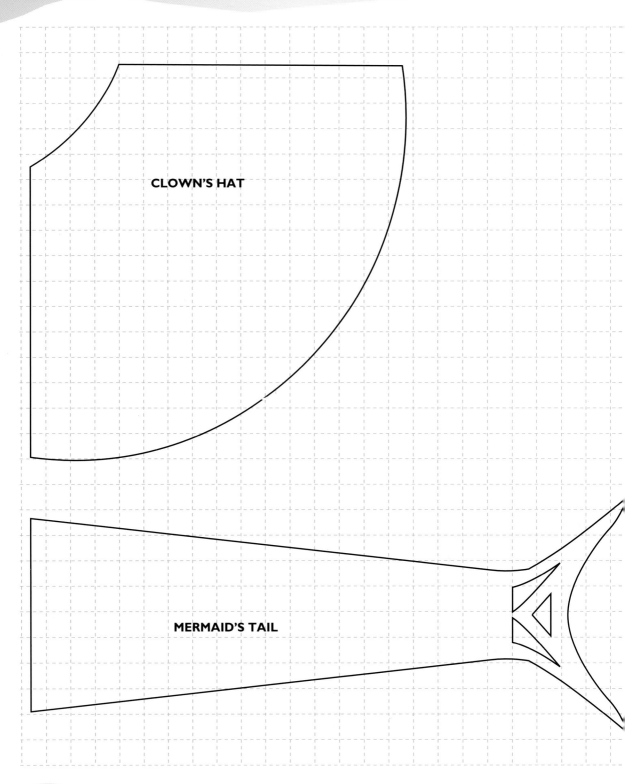

CLOWN'S HAT

MERMAID'S TAIL

FLOWER HEADBANK

BUTTERFLY WING

FLOWER COLLAR

 INDEX